GW01424180

Sip The Rainbow

100 Delicious Juice and Smoothie
Recipes For Vibrant Health

Naya Lizardo

Copyright © 2013 by Naya Lizardo

All rights reserved. This book or any portion thereof may not be reproduced or used in any manner whatsoever without the express written permission of the author except for the use of brief quotations in a book review.
Published in the United States of America

INTRODUCTION I

PART I: NOURISHING RAINBOW 1

Chapter 1: BLUE & PURPLE RULE   3

Chapter 2: GREEN POWERHOUSE   5

Chapter 3: ORANGE & YELLOW   7

Chapter 4 NOURISHING RED   9

Chapter 5: SIMPLY WHITE   11

PART II: BLENDING AND JUICING FOR OPTIMAL HEALTH............................ 13

Chapter 6: Health Benefits of Smoothies   14

Chapter 7: Health Benefits of Juicing   15

PART III: RECIPES FOR VIBRANT HEALTH 17

Chapter 8: BLUE AND PURPLE   19

SMOOTHIES...20

JUICES 29

Chapter 9: GREEN   35

SMOOTHIES...36

JUICES 48

Chapter 10: ORANGE & YELLOW   57

SMOOTHIES...58

JUICES 67

Chapter 11: RED   75

SMOOTHIES...76

JUICES 85

Chapter 12: WHITE   93

SMOOTHIES 94

JUICES.. 104

CONCLUSION 106

ABOUT THE AUTHOR 108

INTRODUCTION

This book is designed to help you better nourish your body with wholesome fruits and vegetables using delicious smoothies and juices that you can easily make at home. Freshly extracted juices and smoothies provide a delectable alternative to the unhealthy "quick fix" and fast food meals that are so common in our western diets. Fruit and vegetables juices and smoothies are the perfect remedy for a less than nutritional diet. Juicing and smoothies can help you clear out toxins, drop excess weight, and improve your health and vitality. Fruit and vegetable smoothies and juices not only enhance your health and improve the overall quality of your life, but they are also deliciously satisfying.

Benefits of incorporating healthy smoothies and freshly extracted juices into your diet:

You will look and feel rejuvenated

Improved focus, clarity, and energy

Clearer, glowing skin

Reduced cravings for sugar, caffeine and fats

Improved self-confidence

Better resistance to disease

More restful sleep

Improved motivation and optimism

Heightened sense of smell, sight, touch, sound, taste

Improved metabolism and enhanced digestion

PART I: NOURISHING RAINBOW

Vegetables and fruits are essential to our health. Our bodies are worn out from working overtime to metabolize a steady diet of processed food. Eliminating processed foods from your diet and replacing them with colorful health boosting foods will let your body return to optimal health.

So what does color have to do with our health anyway? There are thousands health promoting phytochemicals in plant foods and each color fruit and vegetable contains its own unique set of nutrients. By consuming plant foods in a variety of colors, you ensure that you are getting the most complete health benefits. Consuming plenty of colorful fruits and vegetables can help prevent or even reverse a multitude of illnesses and conditions such as heart disease and strokes, high blood pressure and many types of cancers. It is therefore vital that you consume a wide variety of colorful fruits and vegetables every day.

~1~

BLUE & PURPLE RULE

Blue and purple fruits and vegetables contain anthocyanins, flavonoids that not only give these food their color, but also help limit damage caused by free radicals and reduce the risk of high blood pressure, macular degeneration, memory problems, heart disease and cancer. Blue and purple plant foods also contain lutein, resveratrol, vitamin C, fiber, zeaxanthin, ellagic acid, and quercetin. These nutrients support retinal health, boost immune system, improve digestion, improve mineral absorption, reduce inflammation, limit the activity of cancer cells and reduce tumor growth. The darker the hue, the higher the phytochemical concentration.

Blue, violet and indigo foods include:

Black currants

Blackberries

Blueberries

Eggplant

Grapes

Plums

Purple asparagus

Purple cabbage

Purple figs

Purple potatoes

Raisins and prunes

~2~

GREEN POWERHOUSE

Green vegetables have long been hailed as the go-to good-for-you food for a reason; they are nutritional powerhouses. Green plant foods contain chlorophyll which encourages alkaline balance and helps ward off cancer by removing potentially carcinogenic compounds from the body. Green plant foods also contain lutein, zeaxanthin, calcium, folate, vitamin C, calcium, and indoles. Green fruits and vegetables protect against breast and prostate cancers, lower blood pressure and LDL cholesterol levels, improve digestion, fight harmful free-radicals, boost immune system activity and support retinal health and vision.

Green foods include:

Artichokes	Green apples	Lettuce
Asparagus	Green beans	Limes
Avocados	Green cabbage	Mustard greens
Arugula	Green onion	Okra
Broccoli	Green pears	Peas
Broccoli rabe	Green peppers	Spinach
Celery	Kale	Snap peas
Cucumbers	Kiwifruit	Zucchini
Endive	Leeks	

~3~

ORANGE & YELLOW

Yellow and orange fruits and vegetables pack a nutritional punch! They are jam-packed with carotenoids and bioflavanoids, antioxidants which help improve immune system function and lower the risk of heart disease, vision problems and cancer. Yellow and orange fruits and vegetables also contain zeaxanthin, lycopene, vitamin C, potassium and beta-carotene. These nutrient-rich foods promote collagen formation, encourage alkaline balance, fight free radicals, help build healthy bones, reduce the risk of certain cancers, lower LDL (bad) cholesterol and blood pressure levels, and reduce age related macular degeneration.

Yellow and orange foods include:

Apricots

Butternut squash

Cantaloupe

Carrots

Grapefruit

Lemon

Mangoes

Nectarines

Oranges

Papayas

Peaches

Pineapples

Pumpkin

Rutabagas

Sweet corn

Sweet potatoes

Tangerines

Yellow apples

Yellow peppers

Yellow squash

~4~

NOURISHING RED

Red fruits and vegetables are chock-full of tasty, nutritious benefits! They are rich in phytochemicals, such as lycopene and anthocyanins, which help your body fight disease and promote overall good health. Lycopene helps rid the body of damaging free radicals and protects against certain cancers and heart disease. They also delay the aging of cells in the body.

Red foods include:

Beets	Red apples
Red cabbage	Red bell peppers
Cherries	Red chili peppers
Cranberries	Red grapes
Guava	Red onions
Pink/Red grapefruit	Red pears
Pomegranates	Rhubarb
Radicchio	Strawberries
Radishes	Tomatoes
Raspberries	Watermelon

~5~
SIMPLY WHITE

White fruits and vegetables may be lacking in color but they are bursting with powerful phytochemicals which help your body fight disease and promote good health. These phytochemicals help lower your risk for heart disease and cancer. Some white plant foods like garlic, contain allicin, which has been shown to lower the risk for high blood pressure, high cholesterol, heart disease and cancer. These foods contain beta-glucans, EGCG, SDG, and lignans which provide powerful immune boosting activity. White plant foods are also good sources of potassium, vitamin C, folate, niacin and riboflavin.

White foods include:
Bananas
Cauliflower
Garlic
Ginger
Jerusalem artichoke
Jicama
Turnips

PART II: BLENDING AND JUICING FOR OPTIMAL HEALTH

You already know that eating a diet rich in colorful fruits and vegetables is the key to optimal health. You may think that it's challenging enough to eat enough fruits and vegetables without also worrying about incorporating a rainbow of colors into your meals. Fortunately, juicing and blending make it easy to do just that; you can simply Sip The Rainbow.

~6~
Health Benefits of Smoothies

Smoothies can make it super easy for you to incorporate more fruits and vegetables into your diet. Fruit and vegetable smoothies are chock-full of vitamins, minerals, other nourishing phytonutrients and fiber. Smoothies are a simple way to nourish and revitalize your body, improve your digestion and even lose weight.

Fruit and vegetable smoothies can be a side item or a complete meal replacement depending on your goals and caloric needs. You can easily add protein ingredients (such as plain yogurt, almond milk, soy milk or your preferred protein powder) making it a more balanced, nutritious meal. Green smoothies, especially, are a great way to boost vegetable consumption.

Smoothies also promote healthy weight loss. The high fiber content in smoothies helps you feel fuller longer, provides a steady release of nutrients over time and helps prevent blood sugar spikes, helping you to stave off cravings and hunger pains. The fiber also helps keep your digestive tract moving and provides good bacteria needed for proper digestion. If you combine drinking fruits and vegetable smoothies with a sensible diet and consistent exercise, it would be almost impossible for you not to lose unwanted pounds.

~7~
Health Benefits of Juicing

Juicing is a process which extracts water and nutrients from fruits and vegetables by removing the fiber. By removing the fiber, your body has less digestion work to do and is able to quickly absorb more of the nourishing nutrients from the fruits and vegetables. Years of poor diets have left many with impaired digestion and limited ability to absorb the nutrients from the fruit and vegetables we consume. The juicing process can help to break down these fruits and vegetables making their nourishing nutrients more available to your body.

Juicing makes it a lot easier for us to consume more fruits and vegetables. If you ever used a juicer before, you know it takes a lot of fruits and veggies to make one glass of juice. This means that by drinking just a couple glasses of juice, you end up consuming a lot more veggies and fruits than you would normally ever eat in a day. Juicing also makes it easier to consume a wider array of fruits and vegetables resulting in more complete nourishment.

Freshly extracted fruit and vegetables juices provide highly concentrated source of vitamins and minerals which help combat the damaging effects of free radicals, detox your liver and ward off disease, cancer and other degenerative illnesses. These juices also give you a jolt of energy and vitality.

You Don't Have to Choose

Both juicing and blending allow you to incorporate healthy fruits and vegetables into your diet. Many people prefer blending because they feel that keeping the fiber in the juice is important since it helps to avoid spikes in blood sugar. Others prefer juicing because removing the fiber makes the juice easier to digest and allows you to absorb the nutrients faster. But you don't have to choose; incorporating both into your diet will allow you to get the best of both worlds.

PART III: RECIPES FOR VIBRANT HEALTH

The colorful fruits and vegetable juice and smoothies in the recipes below are full of vitamins, minerals and other essential nutrients. All of the juices and smoothies below are simple to make, require very few ingredients and contain no gluten or artificial ingredients. For optimal benefits, the juices and smoothies should be prepared fresh each day. To make the fresh juices, it is best to use a juicer; however if you do not have a juicer, you can make the juices in the blender. Simply put the fruits and vegetables in the blender, add some filtered water and blend. Strain the puree with a cheese cloth or strainer

~8~

BLUE AND PURPLE

Blue and purple fruits and vegetables such as blueberries are jam-packed with flavonoids which improve cardiovascular health, reverse short-term memory loss associated with aging, and improve motor skills

SMOOTHIES

Creamy Blue Treat

With only 80 calories per cup and a plethora of health benefits including vitamin c, manganese, fiber, and antioxidants, blueberries are quite the super food.

1 cup blueberries
1 cup red cabbage
2 medium bananas
2 teaspoons chia seeds, soaked
1 cup water
½ cup almond or soy milk
6-10 ice cubes

Combine all ingredients in a blender and blend until smooth.

Makes 2 servings

~~~~~~~~~~~~~~~~~~~~~~~~~~~~~~

Very Berry Bliss

1 cup coconut milk

1 cup blueberries

½ cup blackberries

2 tablespoons Goji berries

1 tablespoon ground flaxseed

2 dates

6-10 ice cubes

Combine all ingredients in a blender and blend until smooth.

Makes 2 servings

~~~~~~~~~~~~~~~~~~~~~~~~~~~~~~~

Blackberry Banana Blitz

1 medium banana

½ cup blackberries

1 cup orange juice

½ cup soy or almond milk

6-10 ice cubes

Combine all ingredients in a blender and blend until smooth.

Makes 2 servings

~~~~~~~~~~~~~~~~~~~~~~~~~~~~~~~

Blueberry Nirvana

Antioxidant-rich green tea and blueberries makes this smoothie a nutritional powerhouse.

1 cup brewed green tea
2 teaspoons honey
2 cups blueberries
1 banana
1 cup rice milk
6 to 8 ice cubes

Combine all ingredients in a blender and blend until smooth.

Makes 2 servings

~~~~~~~~~~~~~~~~~~~~~~~~~~~~~~

Blueberry Crumble

1 cup almond milk

1 cup oats

1 cup blueberries

1 tablespoon ground flax seeds

½ tablespoon almond extract

Dash of cinnamon

6-8 ice cubes

Combine all ingredients in a blender and blend until smooth.

Makes 2 servings

~~~~~~~~~~~~~~~~~~~~~~~~~~~~~~~~

Triple Berry Supreme

½ cup water

½ cup low fat yogurt

1 cup blueberries

½ cup raspberries

½ cup strawberries

6-8 ice cubes

Combine all ingredients in a blender and blend until smooth.

Makes 2 servings

Grape Madness

Most people don't normally think of grapes when they think of smoothies, but these tiny fruits pack a lot of punch when it comes to nutrition. Grapes contain a nice dose of vitamin C, resveratrol and other healthful antioxidants.

1 ½ cup seedless grapes
½ cup almond milk
½ cup orange juice
1 tablespoon flax seed oil
6-10 ice cubes

Combine all ingredients in a blender and blend until smooth.

Makes 2 servings

~~~~~~~~~~~~~~~~~~~~~~~~~~~~~

Berry Coconut Chiller

1 cup blueberries

½ cup coconut water

½ soy or almond milk

¼ cup shredded coconut (unsweetened)

¼ teaspoon cinnamon

6 to 8 ice cubes

Combine all ingredients in a blender and blend until smooth.

Makes 2 servings

~~~~~~~~~~~~~~~~~~~~~~~~~~~~~~

Blueberry Almond Butter Smoothie

1 cup almond milk

1 cup blueberries

1 banana

2 cups spinach

1 tablespoon almond butter

1 tablespoon flaxseeds

1/4 teaspoon cinnamon

6-10 ice cubes

Combine all ingredients in a blender and blend until smooth.

Makes 2 servings

Blackberry Blast

Blackberries are among the top ranked antioxidant-rich fruits and are also rich in fiber, manganese, copper and vitamin C.

1 cup blackberries
1 banana
½ cup of orange juice
2 cups fresh spinach
1 cup water
6 to 8 ice cubes

Combine all ingredients in a blender and blend until smooth.

Makes 2 servings

~~~~~~~~~~~~~~~~~~~~~~~~~~~~~

Black and Blue Smoothie

1 cup blackberries

1 cup blueberries

1 small apple, cored

1 banana

1 teaspoons flax seeds

1 cup spinach

1 cup water

6-10 ice cubes

Combine all ingredients in a blender and blend until smooth.

Makes 2 servings

~~~~~~~~~~~~~~~~~~~~~~~~~~~~~~

JUICES

Purple Haze

This tasty drink full of bromelain and anthocyanins which reduce inflammation and promote overall health.

3 slices of pineapple
½ cup blueberries
¼ head purple cabbage
1 cucumber
Thumb sized piece of ginger

Process all ingredients in a juicer. Pour over ice, stir and serve.

Makes 2 servings.

~~~~~~~~~~~~~~~~~~~~~~~~~~~~~~~

Orange Blueberry Kicker

2 cups organic blueberries
1 orange
1 lemon

Process all ingredients in a juicer. Pour over ice, stir and serve.

Makes 2 servings.

~~~~~~~~~~~~~~~~~~~~~~~~~~~~~~

Purple Perfection

3 Fuji Apples
1 large Beet with stalk
4 kale leaves
1 cucumber

Process all ingredients in a juicer. Pour over ice, stir and serve.

Makes 2 servings.

~~~~~~~~~~~~~~~~~~~~~~~~~~~~~~

Purple Passion

½ medium purple cabbage

2 cups red seedless grapes

½ medium fresh pineapple

1 passion fruit (pulp and seeds)

Process all ingredients in a juicer. Pour over ice, stir and serve.

Makes 2 servings.

~~~~~~~~~~~~~~~~~~~~~~~~~~~~~~~

Black and Blue

1 cup blueberries
½ cup blackberries
3 cups concord grapes
1 apple
1 thumb size pieces of ginger

Process all ingredients in a juicer. Pour over ice, stir and serve.

Makes 2 servings.

~~~~~~~~~~~~~~~~~~~~~~~~~~~~~~

~9~
GREEN

Green smoothies and juices are awesome! They will do wonders to boost your nutrition, energy levels and help you achieve your weight loss, detox and health goals.

Chaz's - Spinach
Cucumber.
Apple - green x1.
Lime/lemon.

SMOOTHIES

Spirulina Magic

Spirulina is one of the most potent nutrient sources available. It is composed of 62% complete protein. Each spoonful of spirulina powder gives you four grams of complete protein, so you'll get all the essential amino acids.

¼ cup of Spirulina
1 banana
½ cup of plain yogurt
1 cup blueberries
½ cup orange juice
½ cup water
6 to 8 ice cubes

Combine all ingredients in a blender and blend until smooth.

Makes 2 servings

~~~~~~~~~~~~~~~~~~~~~~~~~~~~~~

Green Monster

3 leaves kale, stems removed
3 leaves chard, stems removed
½ bunch dandelion greens
2 kiwis
1 banana
2 cups water

Combine all ingredients in a blender and blend until smooth.

Makes 2 servings

~~~~~~~~~~~~~~~~~~~~~~~~~~~~~

Cool Cucumber

1 large cucumber
2 cups fresh baby spinach
2 pears
½ cup water
1 tablespoon flax seed oil
6 to 8 ice cubes

Combine all ingredients in a blender and blend until smooth.

Makes 2 servings

~~~~~~~~~~~~~~~~~~~~~~~~~~~~~

Awesome Avocado

Avocados are an amazing super food with a rich flavor and powerful wide-ranging health benefits. This tropical tasting smoothie is nutritious and satisfying.

½ avocado
1 banana
½ cup nonfat plain Greek yogurt
1 cup fresh orange juice
2 tablespoons of honey
6-10 ice cubes

Combine all ingredients in a blender and blend until smooth.

Makes 2 servings

~~~~~~~~~~~~~~~~~~~~~~~~~~~~~~

Smooth Avocado Banana

¼ avocado
1 banana
1 cup blueberries
1 cucumber
2 cups spinach
1 cup coconut water
6-10 ice cubes

Combine all ingredients in a blender and blend until smooth.

Makes 2 servings

~~~~~~~~~~~~~~~~~~~~~~~~~~~~~~

Pear Avocado Bliss

1 pear
¼ avocado
1 cup spinach
½ cup coconut water
1 cup almond milk
1 teaspoon chia seeds
1 scoop protein powder
6-10 ice cubes

Combine all ingredients in a blender and blend until smooth.

Makes 2 servings

Green Tropics

This delicious spinach, pineapple and banana smoothie is not only nourishing, but delicious as well.

2 cups of spinach leaves
1 cup of kale
1 large banana
½ cup of pineapple
1 cup water
6-10 ice cubes

Combine all ingredients in a blender and blend until smooth.

Makes 2 servings

~~~~~~~~~~~~~~~~~~~~~~~~~~~~~

Green Protein

1 cup kale
1 cup spinach
1 scoop protein powder
1 pear
½ lemon
½ inch ginger
½ cup coconut water
½ cup water
6-10 ice cubes

Combine all ingredients in a blender and blend until smooth.

Makes 2 servings

~~~~~~~~~~~~~~~~~~~~~~~~~~~~~~

Perfect Broccoli

Broccoli stimulates detoxifying enzymes which help to flush out carcinogens and other toxins from the body.

2 cups broccoli florets
2 celery ribs
2 green apples
Juice of ½ lemon
1 medium banana
1 teaspoon honey
1 cup almond milk
½ cup water

Combine all ingredients in a blender and blend until smooth.

Makes 2 servings

~~~~~~~~~~~~~~~~~~~~~~~~~~~~~~~

Rapid Recovery

Try this tasty smoothie for optimal recovery, energy, and vibrant health.

1 handful of kale
1 handful of spinach
¼ cup parsley
1 tablespoon spirulina
1 scoop of protein powder
½ cup of water
½ almond milk
½ banana
6-10 ice cubes

Combine all ingredients in a blender and blend until smooth.

Makes 2 servings

~~~~~~~~~~~~~~~~~~~~~~~~~~~~~

Jolly Spinach

2 cups spinach

½ cup fresh orange juice

¼ cup fresh raspberries

3 fresh strawberries

½ banana

1 cup almond milk

1 teaspoon honey

6-10 ice cubes

Combine all ingredients in a blender and blend until smooth.

Makes 2 servings

~~~~~~~~~~~~~~~~~~~~~~~~~~~~~

Minty Greens

2 cups spinach

1 cup mango

2 medium ribs celery

1 cup orange juice

¼ cup fresh mint

6-10 ice cubes

Combine all ingredients in a blender and blend until smooth.

Makes 2 servings

Green Ginger Refresher

1 cup of spinach

1 cucumber

2 tablespoon minced ginger

2 apples, cored

Juice of 1 lime

1 teaspoon honey

1 cup water

6-10 ice cubes

Combine all ingredients in a blender and blend until smooth.

Makes 2 servings

~~~~~~~~~~~~~~~~~~~~~~~~~~~~~~

Green Zinger

½ cucumber

1 stalk celery

3 cups leafy greens

3 teaspoon fresh lemon juice

1 apple, cored

1 teaspoon gingerroot

2 cups water

6-10 ice cubes

Combine all ingredients in a blender and blend until smooth.

Makes 2 servings

~~~~~~~~~~~~~~~~~~~~~~~~~~~~~~

JUICES

Kale Cleanser

The celery, kale and parsley that contribute to this juice's bright green color are bursting with nutrition and help flush out toxins from your system.

2 cups kale
1 cup parsley
2 celery stalks
3 cups romaine
1 cucumber
2 apples

Process all ingredients in a juicer. Pour over ice, stir and serve.

Makes 2 servings

~~~~~~~~~~~~~~~~~~~~~~~~~~~~~~

Sweet and Savory

With perfectly balanced sweet and savory flavors, this juice blend is very detoxifying.

5 medium carrots
3 celery stalks
4 medium kale leaves
5 Swiss chard leaves
3 apples

Process all ingredients in a juicer. Pour over ice, stir and serve.

Makes 2 servings

~~~~~~~~~~~~~~~~~~~~~~~~~~~~~~

Apple Kiwi Zinger

4 apples

6 kiwis

1 lemon

Process all ingredients in a juicer. Pour over ice, stir and serve.

Makes 2 servings

~~~~~~~~~~~~~~~~~~~~~~~~~~~~

Zesty Kale Apple

2 celery stalks

1 cucumber

3 apples

1 lemon

3 kale leaves

1 inch piece of fresh ginger

Process all ingredients in a juicer. Pour over ice, stir and serve.

Makes 2 servings

~~~~~~~~~~~~~~~~~~~~~~~~~~~~

Veggie Magic

4 carrots

3 apples

2 celery stalks

1 handful wheatgrass

1 handful parsley

Process all ingredients in a juicer. Pour over ice, stir and serve.

Makes 2 servings

~~~~~~~~~~~~~~~~~~~~~~~~~~~~~

Cucumber Tonic

1 cucumber

4 kale leaves

4 carrots

1 beet with greens

1 apple

Process all ingredients in a juicer. Pour over ice, stir and serve.

Makes 2 servings.

~~~~~~~~~~~~~~~~~~~~~~~~~~~~~

Nourishing Broccoli

8 broccoli florets

6 carrots

2 apples

Process all ingredients in a juicer. Pour over ice, stir and serve.

Makes 2 servings

~~~~~~~~~~~~~~~~~~~~~~~~~~~~~~

Cucumber Lemon Quencher

1 cucumber

½ lemon

1 apple

½ green chard leaf

5 kale leaves

1 cup spinach

2 stalks celery

1 thumb sized piece of ginger

Process all ingredients in a juicer. Pour over ice, stir and serve.

Makes 2 servings

~~~~~~~~~~~~~~~~~~~~~~~~~~~~~~

Kiwi Perfection

1 large celery stalk
1 apples
2 kiwis
1/3 cup parsley
1 tablespoon ginger
½ lime

Process all ingredients in a juicer. Pour over ice, stir and serve.

Makes 2 servings

~~~~~~~~~~~~~~~~~~~~~~~~~~~~~

Zesty Grapefruit Kale

5 kale leaves
1 grapefruit
3-4 celery stalks
1 apple
1 cucumber
1 lime

Process all ingredients in a juicer. Pour over ice, stir and serve.

Makes 2 servings

~~~~~~~~~~~~~~~~~~~~~~~~~~~~~

Mellow Romaine

6 romaine lettuce leaves

2 pears

2 celery stalks

5 kale leaves

1 lemon

Process all ingredients in a juicer. Pour over ice, stir and serve.

Makes 2 servings

~~~~~~~~~~~~~~~~~~~~~~~~~~~~~~

~10~
ORANGE & YELLOW

Bright yellow and orange fruits and vegetables can be an instant mood booster. Yellow and orange hues represent energy, happiness and joy. The smoothies and juices in this section will lift your spirits while nourishing your body, mind and soul

.

SMOOTHIES

Peaches and Cream

This delicious smoothie is loaded with phytonutrients, vitamins, minerals and enzymes.

1 peach, pit removed
½ cup vanilla yogurt
1 frozen banana
½ teaspoon stevia
6 to 8 ice cubes

Combine all ingredients in a blender and blend until smooth.

Makes 2 servings

~~~~~~~~~~~~~~~~~~~~~~~~~~~~

Creamy Carrot Perfection

10 baby carrots
½ banana
½ cup orange juice
6 to 8 ice cubes
1 cup plain nonfat yogurt

Combine all ingredients in a blender and blend until smooth.

Makes 2 servings

~~~~~~~~~~~~~~~~~~~~~~~~~~~~~~

Orange Sunrise

This tangy sweet blend is healthy and delicious.

2 apricots
2 carrots
½ cup mango
1 cup papaya
1 cup orange juice
6 to 8 ice cubes

Combine all ingredients in a blender and blend until smooth.

Makes 2 servings

Pineapple Papaya Soother

Pineapple and papayas contain enzymes that digest proteins and help soothe the upset stomachs. The live cultures in the yogurt also help digestion.

1 cup papaya
½ cup pineapple
1 cup plain yogurt
Juice from ½ lime
1 tablespoon honey

Combine all ingredients in a blender and blend until smooth.

Makes 2 servings

~~~~~~~~~~~~~~~~~~~~~~~~~~~~~~

Creamy Dreamy Pineapple

1 cup pineapple chunks

½ cup of coconut water

½ cup plain yogurt

½ cup kale

½ banana

6 to 8 ice cubes

Garnish with unsweetened coconut flakes

Combine all ingredients in a blender and blend until smooth.

Makes 2 servings

~~~~~~~~~~~~~~~~~~~~~~~~~~~~~~

Pineapple Kiwi Colada

1 kiwi fruit

1 cup pineapple chunks

1 cup raw spinach

¼ cup grated coconut

1 cup water

6 to 8 ice cubes

Combine all ingredients in a blender and blend until smooth.

Makes 2 servings

Mango Tango

This delicious smoothie is packed with healthy vitamins including beta-carotene.

1 mango, chopped

6 baby carrots

1 cup water

6 to 8 ice cubes

Dash of nutmeg

Combine all ingredients in a blender and blend until smooth.

Makes 2 servings

~~~~~~~~~~~~~~~~~~~~~~~~~~~~~~

Simply Papaya

1 cup papaya
1 cup rice milk
1 teaspoon honey
Sprinkle of cinnamon
6 to 8 ice cubes

Combine all ingredients in a blender and blend until smooth.

Makes 2 servings

~~~~~~~~~~~~~~~~~~~~~~~~~~~~~~

Orange Sublime

A low-calorie, healthy smoothie that tastes sublime. A perfect breakfast or mid-afternoon snack.

2 navel oranges
½ cup plain low fat yogurt
¼ cup orange juice
½ teaspoon vanilla extract
6 to 8 ice cubes

Combine all ingredients in a blender and blend until smooth.

Makes 2 servings

Pumpkin Pie Delight

This delicious healthy smoothie is rich in vitamin A, potassium and fiber.

1 cup pumpkin chunks or purée
1 banana
1 cup soy or almond milk
1 teaspoon honey
½ teaspoon pure vanilla extract
Dash of cinnamon and nutmeg
6 to 8 ice cubes

Combine all ingredients in a blender and blend until smooth.

Makes 2 servings

~~~~~~~~~~~~~~~~~~~~~~~~~~~~~

Pineapple Passion Potion

1 cup pineapple, cubed

3 passion fruits, inner fruit only

1 medium banana

1 cup fresh baby spinach

8 ounces coconut water

6 to 8 ice cubes

Combine all ingredients in a blender and blend until smooth.

Makes 2 servings

~~~~~~~~~~~~~~~~~~~~~~~~~~~~~

Spiced Carrot Cake

1 cup carrot

1 cup pineapple

½ cup coconut milk

½ cup orange juice

¼ teaspoon ground cinnamon

¼ teaspoon ground nutmeg

¼ teaspoon ground ginger

Combine all ingredients in a blender and blend until smooth.

Makes 2 servings

JUICES

Carrot Lettuce Cleanser

This sweet and delicious juice is very cleansing.

5 large carrots

3 apples

3 celery stalks

4 romaine lettuce leaves

4 red lettuce leaves

Process all ingredients in a juicer. Pour over ice, stir and serve.

Makes 2 servings.

~~~~~~~~~~~~~~~~~~~~~~~~~~~~~~~

Lime Orange Cooler

4 navel oranges, outer rind removed
1 lime, outer rind removed
¼ cup sparkling water

Process all ingredients in a juicer. Pour over ice, stir and serve.

Makes 2 servings.

~~~~~~~~~~~~~~~~~~~~~~~~~~~~~

Carrot Apple Tang

6 carrots
3 apples
3 red bell pepper
3 romaine lettuce
1 lemon, outer rind removed

Process all ingredients in a juicer. Pour over ice, stir and serve.

Makes 2 servings.

~~~~~~~~~~~~~~~~~~~~~~~~~~~~~

Eye Opener

1 grapefruit

3 navel oranges

Process all ingredients in a juicer. Pour over ice, stir and serve.

Makes 2 servings.

~~~~~~~~~~~~~~~~~~~~~~~~~~~~

Carrot Kale Detox Juice

2 oranges

1 lemon

5 carrots

2 cups chopped kale

½ inch of fresh ginger root

Process all ingredients in a juicer. Pour over ice, stir and serve.

Makes 2 servings.

~~~~~~~~~~~~~~~~~~~~~~~~~~~~

Pineapple Grape Cocktail

1 bunch green grapes
½ cup pineapple chunks
1 lemon

Process all ingredients in a juicer. Pour over ice, stir and serve.

Makes 2 servings.

~~~~~~~~~~~~~~~~~~~~~~~~~~~~~~~

Tropical Nectar

1 cup pineapple chunks
6 strawberries
1 mango

Process all ingredients in a juicer. Pour over ice, stir and serve.

Makes 2 servings.

~~~~~~~~~~~~~~~~~~~~~~~~~~~~~~~

Carrot-Beet

10 carrots

1 beet with greens

Process all ingredients in a juicer. Pour over ice, stir and serve.

Makes 2 servings

~~~~~~~~~~~~~~~~~~~~~~~~~~~~~

Spicy Hearty Carrot

7 carrots

2 large tomatoes

1 red bell peppers

3 cloves garlic

4 stalks celery

1 cup watercress

1 cup spinach

½ jalapeño (optional)

Process all ingredients in a juicer. Pour over ice, stir and serve.

Makes 2 servings.

~~~~~~~~~~~~~~~~~~~~~~~~~~~~~

Summer Cocktail

2 oranges

½ mango

3 slice of fresh pineapple

1 slice of watermelon

Process all ingredients in a juicer. Pour over ice, stir and serve.

~~~~~~~~~~~~~~~~~~~~~~~~~~~~~

Rise and Shine

4 apples

8 carrots

3 celery stalks

Process all ingredients in a juicer. Pour over ice, stir and serve.

~~~~~~~~~~~~~~~~~~~~~~~~~~~~~

Carrot Cantaloupe

8 carrots

¼ of cantaloupe

Process all ingredients in a juicer. Pour over ice, stir and serve.

~~~~~~~~~~~~~~~~~~~~~~~~~~~~~

Recipes make 2 servings

~11~
RED

From pomegranates to beets, red fruits and vegetables pack a vibrant nutritional punch. The smoothies and juices included in this section feature red produce such strawberries, cherries, raspberries, watermelon, tomatoes, and beets and are loaded with powerful antioxidants. These juices and smoothies can help you lower your risk of heart disease and stroke, as well as macular degeneration, the leading cause of blindness in people 60 or older.

SMOOTHIES

Pomegranate Watermelon Refresher

½ cup of pomegranate seeds
2 heaping cups fresh watermelon chunks
½ cup water
6-10 ice cubes

Combine all ingredients in a blender and blend until smooth.

Makes 2 servings

~~~~~~~~~~~~~~~~~~~~~~~~~~~~~~

Strawberry Almond Smoothie

1 cup strawberries
1 cup almond milk
2 tablespoons almond butter

Combine all ingredients in a blender and blend until smooth.

Makes 2 servings

~~~~~~~~~~~~~~~~~~~~~~~~~~~~~~

Watermelon Wonder

Juicy watermelon are rich in powerful disease-fighting lycopene and antioxidants.

2 cups watermelon chunks
1 small banana, chopped
6-10 ice cubes
1 cup plain yogurt

Combine all ingredients in a blender and blend until smooth.

Makes 2 servings

~~~~~~~~~~~~~~~~~~~~~~~~~~~~~~

Strawberry Banana Supreme

6 strawberries
1 banana
1 cup plain nonfat yogurt
½ cup orange juice
6 to 8 ice cubes

Combine all ingredients in a blender and blend until smooth.

Makes 2 servings

~~~~~~~~~~~~~~~~~~~~~~~~~~~~~

Cranberry Cleanser

1 cup cranberries
2 large celery stalk
1 cucumber
2 apples
1 pear
1 cup spinach

Combine all ingredients in a blender and blend until smooth.

Makes 2 servings

~~~~~~~~~~~~~~~~~~~~~~~~~~~~~

Tropical Guava Twist

Guavas are especially rich in vitamin C with ½ cup of guava containing about 209% RDA. Guavas are also a great source of vitamin A and folate.

½ cup red guava, seeds removed
4 fresh strawberries
1 cup pineapple
1 teaspoon fresh lemon juice
1 cup water
6-10 ice cubes

Combine all ingredients in a blender and blend until smooth.

Makes 2 servings

~~~~~~~~~~~~~~~~~~~~~~~~~~~~~~~

Berries and Lime

4 fresh strawberries

½ cup fresh raspberries

1 banana

1 cup plain yogurt

½ cup orange juice

1 tablespoon fresh lime juice

6-10 ice cubes

Combine all ingredients in a blender and blend until smooth.

Makes 2 servings

~~~~~~~~~~~~~~~~~~~~~~~~~~~~~~

Cherry Vanilla

1 cup vanilla almond or soymilk milk

8 fresh cherries

1 banana

2 fresh strawberries

1 teaspoon honey

1 scoop vanilla protein powder

Combine all ingredients in a blender and blend until smooth.

Makes 2 servings

Chocolate Covered Strawberries

Believe it or not, this smoothie is yummy and healthy too. Chocolate and strawberries are a dynamite combination! This delicious smoothie will give you boost of energy because it's loaded with vitamins and minerals and it surely satisfy that chocolate craving too!

1 medium banana

8 strawberries

1 tablespoon unsweetened cacao powder

1 ½ cup almond milk

½ cup baby spinach

1 scoop chocolate protein powder

6-10 ice cubes

Combine all ingredients in a blender and blend until smooth.

Makes 2 servings

~~~~~~~~~~~~~~~~~~~~~~~~~~~~~~

Raspberry Joy

1 cup raspberries
1 cup almond or rice milk
¼ cup pitted cherries
½ tablespoon honey
2 teaspoon finely grated fresh ginger
1 teaspoon ground flaxseed
2 teaspoon fresh lemon juice

Combine all ingredients in a blender and blend until smooth.

Makes 2 servings

~~~~~~~~~~~~~~~~~~~~~~~~~~~~~~~

Sparkling Cranberries

¼ cup cranberries
1 cup orange juice
½ cup sparkling water
1 cup raspberries
Stevia to taste
6-10 ice cubes

Combine all ingredients in a blender and blend until smooth.

Makes 2 servings

~~~~~~~~~~~~~~~~~~~~~~~~~~~~~~~

Razzle Dazzle

Control your appetite with a delicious mix of peanut butter and raspberries. The raspberries activates on detoxifying enzymes and the ginger stimulates digestion.

1 cup raspberries
½ cup of vanilla yogurt
½ cup water
2 teaspoons honey
1 tablespoon peanut butter
2 teaspoons fresh ginger
6 to 8 ice cubes

Combine all ingredients in a blender and blend until smooth.

Makes 2 servings

~~~~~~~~~~~~~~~~~~~~~~~~~~~~~~

JUICES

Watermelon Cooler

Watermelon and cucumbers are both refreshing and cleansing for the whole body, especially the kidneys. This delicious juice is rich in vitamin A (beta-carotene) and vitamin C.

3 cups watermelon
1 cucumber

Process all ingredients in a juicer. Pour over ice, stir and serve.

Makes 2 servings.

~~~~~~~~~~~~~~~~~~~~~~~~~~~~~~

Cranberry Pear

6 large pears, cored and sliced

2 cups of fresh cranberries

Process all ingredients in a juicer. Pour over ice, stir and serve.

Makes 2 servings.

~~~~~~~~~~~~~~~~~~~~~~~~~~~~~~

Cucumber Beet Coconut

2 cucumbers

½ beet

2 beet greens

2 cups of coconut water

Process all ingredients in a juicer, except the coconut water. Pour over ice, stir and serve.

Makes 2 servings.

~~~~~~~~~~~~~~~~~~~~~~~~~~~~~

Sweet and Fruity

The antioxidant properties and tannins in red grapes help reduce the risk of heart disease and lower cholesterol. Here's a tasty way to enjoy these benefits.

4 cups red grapes

12 strawberries

Process all ingredients in a juicer. Pour over ice, stir and serve.

Makes 2 servings.

~~~~~~~~~~~~~~~~~~~~~~~~~~~~~~~

Pretty in Pink

1 medium pomegranate
3 Fuji apples
3 cups of red grapes
½ lime

Process all ingredients in a juicer. Pour over ice, stir and serve.

Makes 2 servings.

~~~~~~~~~~~~~~~~~~~~~~~~~~~~~~

Tomato Cabbage

1 tomato
2 cups cabbage
4 celery stalks

Process all ingredients in a juicer. Pour over ice, stir and serve.

Makes 2 servings

~~~~~~~~~~~~~~~~~~~~~~~~~~~~~~

Peppery Goodness

3 apples

½ red pepper, deseeded

1 large beetroot

½ lemon, peeled

Process all ingredients in a juicer. Pour over ice, stir and serve.

Makes 2 servings.

~~~~~~~~~~~~~~~~~~~~~~~~~~~~~

Tart and Sweet

5 pears

1 cup of cranberries

Process all ingredients in a juicer. Pour over ice, stir and serve.

Makes 2 servings.

~~~~~~~~~~~~~~~~~~~~~~~~~~~~~

Juicy Perfection

½ small watermelon

3 pomegranates

½ lemon

1 cup raspberries

Process all ingredients in a juicer. Pour over ice, stir and serve.

Makes 2 servings.

~~~~~~~~~~~~~~~~~~~~~~~~~~~~~~

~12~
WHITE

Don't think that just because the foods covered in this section are pale in color, they are lacking in nutrients! On the contrary, the fruits and vegetables used in the following recipes are rich in phytochemicals, vitamins and minerals.

SMOOTHIES

Silky Chai

This delightful alternative to spiced chai latte is packed with antioxidants.

1 banana
½ cup of coconut meat
1 teaspoon ground ginger
1 teaspoon cinnamon
1 teaspoon cloves
1 teaspoon cardamom
2 cups almond milk
6-10 ice cubes

Combine all ingredients in a blender and blend until smooth.

Makes 2 servings

~~~~~~~~~~~~~~~~~~~~~~~~~~~~~~

Coconut Delight

1 Banana

1 cup of fresh coconut meat

1 teaspoon of ground ginger

1 teaspoon ground cloves

A few drops of pure vanilla extract

2 cups of almond milk

6-10 ice cubes

Combine all ingredients in a blender and blend until smooth.

Makes 2 servings

~~~~~~~~~~~~~~~~~~~~~~~~~~~~~

Thick and Creamy

1 cup plain yogurt

1 banana

1 tablespoons honey

2 tablespoons orange juice

1 tablespoon almond butter

6-10 ice cubes

Combine all ingredients in a blender and blend until smooth.

Makes 2 servings~~~~~~~~~~~~~~~~~~~~~~~~~~~~~~

Banana Nut

This delicious blend is rich in potassium which helps combat water weight, vitamins B5 and B6 which promote energy and healthy metabolism. Makes a satisfying snack or meal that will fuel your body, keep you focused and satisfy your hunger for hours.

2 bananas
2 tablespoons of almond butter
1 ½ cups of almond milk
6-10 ice cubes

Combine all ingredients in a blender and blend until smooth.

Makes 2 servings

~~~~~~~~~~~~~~~~~~~~~~~~~~~~~~

Sensuous Pear

This wonderful combination of pears and spices creates a deliciously sensual experience. This smoothie is rich in magnesium which helps boost your metabolism.

2 pears
1 teaspoon ground ginger
1 teaspoon cloves
1 teaspoon allspice
1 ½ cups of water
6-10 ice cubes

Combine all ingredients in a blender and blend until smooth.

Makes 2 servings

~~~~~~~~~~~~~~~~~~~~~~~~~~~~~

Sea Breeze Sensation

This tropical blend combines the tart flavors of citrus with the sweetness of coconut, pineapple and banana for a delightful nutrient packed smoothie.

1 whole white grapefruit
1 banana
½ cup coconut meat
½ cup pineapple
½ cup coconut milk
½ cup almond milk
6-10 ice cubes

Combine all ingredients in a blender and blend until smooth.

Makes 2 servings

~~~~~~~~~~~~~~~~~~~~~~~~~~~~~~~~

Vanilla Bean

¼ cup macadamia nuts

1 banana

1 vanilla bean, seeds scraped

¼ teaspoon vanilla extract

1 cup water

1 cup vanilla almond or soy milk

6-10 ice cubes

Combine all ingredients in a blender and blend until smooth.

Makes 2 servings

~~~~~~~~~~~~~~~~~~~~~~~~~~~~~

Ginger Mint Zing

1 cup papaya

1 teaspoon fresh ginger

4 sprigs fresh mint

1 tablespoon fresh lemon juice

½ cup nonfat Greek yogurt

½ tablespoon honey

Combine all ingredients in a blender and blend until smooth.

Makes 2 servings

Pineapple Cauliflower Splendor

High in vitamin C, cauliflower is mild-tasting vegetable easily masked by fruit flavors.

1 cup cauliflower
1 cup pineapple chunks
1 ripe banana
½ cup low fat yogurt
1 cup soy or almond milk
6 to 8 ice cubes

Combine all ingredients in a blender and blend until smooth.

Makes 2 servings

~~~~~~~~~~~~~~~~~~~~~~~~~~~~~

Smooth Operator

5 raw almonds

1 yellow apple

2 bananas

½ cup natural Greek yogurt

½ cup almond milk

1 teaspoon ground flax

½ teaspoon ground cinnamon

Combine all ingredients in a blender and blend until smooth.

Makes 2 servings

~~~~~~~~~~~~~~~~~~~~~~~~~~~~~

Banana Lemon Tort

1 lemon

1 banana

1 whole kiwi

1 cup almond milk

1 teaspoon honey

Combine all ingredients in a blender and blend until smooth.

Makes 2 servings

~~~~~~~~~~~~~~~~~~~~~~~~~~~~~

Spiced Apple

If you like apple pie but prefer healthier alternatives, you'll love this nutritious smoothie. This smoothie is so tasty that you'll soon forget that it's actually healthy for you.

2 apples
1 teaspoon of ground cinnamon
1 teaspoon of cloves
1 teaspoon of ground ginger
1 cup of natural apple juice
6-10 ice cubes

Combine all ingredients in a blender and blend until smooth.

Makes 2 servings

~~~~~~~~~~~~~~~~~~~~~~~~~~~~~~~

JUICES

Morning Glory

3 gala apples

½ head cauliflower

Combine all ingredients in a blender and blend until smooth.

~~~~~~~~~~~~~~~~~~~~~~~~~~~~~~

Parsnip Surprise

3 parsnips

4 sticks celery

4 medium pears

Combine all ingredients in a blender and blend until smooth.

~~~~~~~~~~~~~~~~~~~~~~~~~~~~~~

Pear Grape Sweetness

1 cup of green grapes

1 pear

1 lime

Combine all ingredients in a blender and blend until smooth.

~~~~~~~~~~~~~~~~~~~~~~~~~~~~~~

Recipes Make 2 servings

CONCLUSION

Thank you for buying and reading this book. I sincerely hope that you found this book to be a valuable resource and that you've enjoyed the recipes.

If you liked this book and would like to share a few words about it with other readers, you can click here to [leave your feedback](). Your thoughts and comments will be very much appreciated.

Thanks again and best wishes!

Naya

Legal Disclaimer

The information provided in this book is designed to provide helpful information regarding the subjects discussed. While best efforts have been used in preparing this book, the author makes no representations or warranties of any kind and assumes no liabilities of any kind with respect to the accuracy or completeness of the contents. The author is not responsible for any specific health or allergy needs that may require medical supervision and is not liable for any damages or negative consequences from any treatment, action, application or preparation, to any person reading or following the information in this book.

Although the foods in this book do contain many health and medicinal properties, they should not be used as a substitute for any medications prescribed to you by your doctor or as a replacement for a doctor's care. You should talk to your doctor before starting any course of therapy or any other treatment.

ABOUT THE AUTHOR

Naya Lizardo is a freelance translator and writer. She has a passion for health, nutrition, and natural medicines, with a special interest in the areas of detoxing, nutritional healing and herbal therapies.

After years of reading and research on a wide range of health disorders and treatments, Naya decided to write her own books that help promote healthy living. Naya is a strong advocate of nutrition as preventive medicine and believes that eating a diet consisting of wholesome, unprocessed foods is key to good health. Through her books, she aims to help her readers reclaim their health and zest for life — to heal their body, mind and spirit through nutritional and alternative therapies.

She is the author of HEALING FOODS: Practical Guide to the Health Benefits and Medicinal Uses of Food, SKINNY DETOX: Eat Your Way to Vibrant Health and Lasting Weight Loss, The FREELANCE TRANSLATION HANDBOOK, and REAL CLEVER SOLUTIONS AND IDEAS with tips and tricks for the home, health, dyi beauty, savvy travel and more.

She lives in sunny Florida with her husband and family. When she's not hard at work writing or translating, she spends her time reading, enjoying the Florida outdoors, traveling, and caring for her home and family.

Connect with Naya Lizardo
Website: www.NayaLizardo.com
Blog: http://forvibranthealth.wordpress.com
Twitter: http://Twitter.com/nayalizardo
Amazon Author Page: http://amzn.to/10T8oQD

4068196R00066

Printed in Great Britain
by Amazon.co.uk, Ltd.,
Marston Gate.